DEAN WHITNEY

Author of Zero to Social - CEO of Dean Whitney Interactive

Sex & Social Media

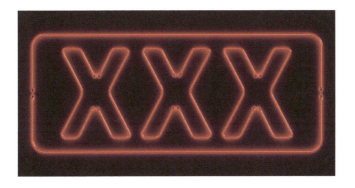

Sex & Social Media examines the effective pick-up artist and how it applies to new marketing in the age of social media.

Sex & Social Media

How marketers can learn from the pick-up artist

Volume 1

ISBN 1452830754

EAN-13 9781452830759

Primary Category

Business & Economics / Marketing / General

Published by Aericon Media - www.aericon.com

Published in the United States

C O N T E N T S

Introduction

Just as social interaction has evolved over the years, so has marketing. Consumer behavior has changed and social media is at the heart of it.

- There are more than 200 million blogs

- 34% of bloggers post opinions about products and services

- 78% of consumers trust peer recommendation.

- 3,000,000 Tweets every day on Twitter.com

You don't need to be a statistician to realize your customers are going on line to find products, gather information, share information, form opinions and select service providers. If you want them to select you, GET IN THE GAME!

Pick-up lines that worked for hipsters fall flat today just as marketing tactics of the the 80's rarely earn customers in the Facebook age. It seems a lot less successful pick-up artists are spouting Austin Powers pick-up lines while marketers seem quite content in going for the quick hit in their attempts at customer acquisition.

Today's playing field has changed and requires a different approach. Sex & Social Media examines the effective pick-up artist and how tricks of that trade apply to new marketing in the age of social media.

Its all about me

The classic old school marketer in today's climate often makes the age old mistake of assuming their audience is very interested in them and their product. They begin the conversation with an impressive list of amazing attributes. Notice we say conversation here, when in fact, this marketer is barely interested in a two-way back and forth.

The marketer has one thing in mind which is acquiring this person as a customer. So the list of attributes are all things that would benefit that deal.

This technique works about as well as if our pick-up artist approached a girl in a club and started listing all of his attributes that could benefit the deal he's trying to close. "Hey there, I have great muscle tone, I smell good and shave my...".

This "all about me" approach doesn't work in relationships. In the nightclub or the marketplace its all about relationships - And by extension, listening.

Its all about you

Imagine the classic series of artist sketches linking the early primitive life forms through those that walk upright. The same line can be drawn from the guy blasting out direct mail pieces to a social media wizard. The slightly more evolved marketer of the 90's read the Zig Ziglar and Dale Carnegie books and a seemingly major epiphany: People don't care about me. So they tweak their lines of communication. Marketing gurus make poignant proclamations like WIIFM (What's in it for me).

This approach, although slightly better, is much like our pick-up artist approaching a candidate and immediately saying "Hey, you're pretty, have a boyfriend?, how would you like to come to my place for some champagne and...".

It's taking a huge leap to assume the prospect has the same end in mind as you do. What if it turns out this girl is an influencer to potential target customer? Okay, she has friends. Smart beautiful friends. And lots of them. Did we miss a chance to engage? People are much more influenced by friends, peers and those they respect and assume are not selling them something so we need to begin more broadly and let the target guide the conversation.

Get them asking questions and looking to you for information. Do this by creating compelling content consistently over time. Maybe this content is not the type which steers leads into your web. Perhaps this is a source of solid useful input which relates to an over-all sector or niche. Its all about attraction - not promotion.

It starts with awareness

Why is it so easy for celebrities to make deals (business or romantic)? Its because the prospect is typically quite familiar with the image, or their perception of that celebrity. People feel a high level of intimacy with an artist through familiarity with their work. Musicians and actors perform at a highly emotional level to an extremely emotional audience of young people racing with new found hormones. Regardless of their social tact these celebrities find swarms of people interested in 'doing business'.

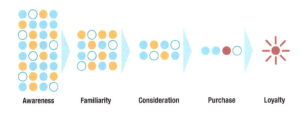

| Awareness | Familiarity | Consideration | Purchase | Loyalty |

McKinsey Quarterly report - The consumer decision journey

Regardless of their social tact these celebrities find swarms of people interested in 'doing business'.

Scoring Big

So how do we create familiarity that leads to a purchase and repeat business (the ultimate score) in today's marketplace? Now that we know the pick-up lines aren't so effective we should look at modern relationships. What does the successful pick-up artist in todays business do to initiate the customer acquisition process?

The whole way consumers are thinking about making purchases, be it a pair of shoes or a car is in the midst of a macro-level overhaul. In "The Consumer Decision Journey," a recent piece put out by the esteemed McKinsey Quarterly Report, the finding concluded that

"Consumers are moving outside the purchasing funnel-changing the way they research and buy your products."

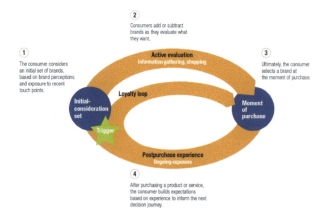

McKinsey Quarterly report - The consumer decision journey

If your marketing hasn't changed in response, it should. Smart business must place greater emphasis on the post-purchase experience. This isn't limited to customer service or customer relations programs. You may think your sector allows for anonymity. Think again, as this is a connected and therefore small world. Your customers see you in the marketplace, subscribe to your e-newsletters read other comments regarding you, perhaps use your product.There are many ongoing touch points. This is what the pick-up artist refers to as "friends with benefits".

Playing the Field

So today's social media pick-up artist really needs to play the field and build a level of awareness and familiarity across channels and venues. This is a way of creating a portfolio of connections so that he is 'top of mind' at the moment of need.

The moment of need

The moment of need in the consumer decision cycle happens when a decision maker needs to pull the trigger on a product or service. The journey from deciding this has to be done to the actual purchase can vary greatly in each case. This is why brand reach and awareness is so important. So that in the moment of need you are top of mind for the customer or someone they are networked with or both. Word-of-mouth recommendations are powerful.

Choosing your territories

Just like the pick-up artist we need to seek out the places where our target audience goes. He doesn't put a sign on his bedroom door and expect the ladies to line up. He seeks out the right venues. That doesn't mean bars and nightclubs. That is about the same as banner ads; they are noisy, disruptive and there's far too much competition for your audience's attention.

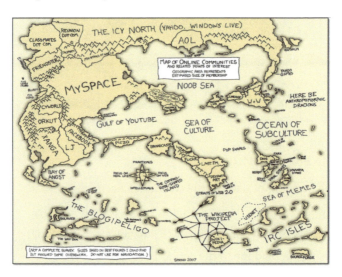

The expert finds places where his audience already spends time and there's a chance for a quality connection. Coffee shops, acting classes, volunteer programs, our pick-up artist is everywhere he may find lovely ladies and have the chance for meaningful dialogue.

Which social networks to target

So, the trick is not to get overwhelmed with the possible destinations in the social media orbit. Wikipedia has a list of social networking sites that most likely includes sites you've never heard of with millions of members.

http://en.wikipedia.org/wiki/List_of_social_networking_websites

While it can be important to find the social networks that are most popular with your audience you should also target the most popular social networks.

Doing this helps you reach the most people possible in the target buyer's network. This also helps to build your search engine authority as you begin to build mentions or buzz across these popular sites. How? Because the amount of linkage is affects search engine authority.

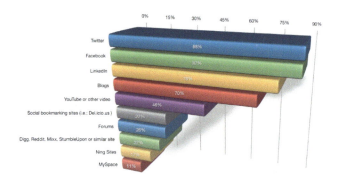

2010 Social Media Marketing Industry Report by Mike Stelzner

By a long shot, Twitter, Facebook, LinkedIn and blogs were the top four social media tools used by marketers. Make time in your day to research the most visited and useful blogs and websites that address the space in which you do business. Start adding comments at the bottom of posts you like and tweeting links to other peoples content. You become a player.

The Art of the Pick-up

Okay. So far, we have learned not to talk about ourselves and not to talk about the customer - so what do we talk about? Ben Franklin said "Either write something worth reading or do something worth writing." Focus on adding value and delivering quality to the marketplace. Do that by generating content that brings value to readers and by participating in activities that people feel compelled to write about.

Yes, a few guys still score using Austin Powers one-liners, but those ranks are thinning rapidly. They have learned to think a bit more long-term while a fair share of marketers still seem quite content in going for the quick hit in their attempts at customer acquisition. Today's playing field has changed and requires a different approach. Sex & Social Media examines the effective pick-up artist and how his new way of approaching the game applies to new marketing in the age of social media.

Know your audience

In *"Crossing the Chasm"* Geoffrey Moore illustrates a curve that represents a brand's audience and how a product or service needs to cross over market penetration from innovators and early adopters to eventually reach the majority and be successful. In essence, how can a brand gain so much steam that it becomes the standard bearer for an item. He also said when you are too far ahead of the market, you're in a chasm. So you need to develop niche markets and create what he called "Beachheads," to carry you until your main market catches up.

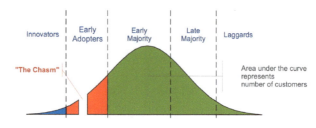

Crossing the Chasm (1991, revised 1999) by Geoffrey A. Moore

This is a useful concept for understanding your social media audience. In the past, marketers and pick-up

---

artists alike would focus on the majority. Mass marketing using television ads and portal ads on sites like MSN and Yahoo are becoming less effective. Why? People are TIVO'ing and fast forwarding past commercials. When was the last time you watched a commercial voluntarily on TV besides Super Bowl Sunday? Exactly. People have become immune to banner ads and as a reflex, mentally block them out. Many even use ad blocker software to avoid banner ads.

Jacob Nielsen's 1-9-90 rule suggest that 90% of users are lurkers who never contribute, 9% of users contribute a little, and 1% of users account for almost all the action.

This 10% represents what Moore calls our "innovators" and "early adopters". Think about all the people you know that own cars, that can drive or may drive some day. They are all the target audience for the automobile industry. How many of these people would you ask for advice about buying a car? Those are the early adopters and innovators that are highly influential.

Engaging the influencers requires sophisticated approach. To accomplish this lofty goal, you need to become an authentic subject matter expert and a true advocate of your brand. Much of your interactions with those influencers will be promoting their content, retweeting their twitter updates, commenting on their blogs and putting links to their content on Twitter. If you are creating genuine content there should be a quid pro quo.

Conversation Starters - Developing Campaigns

So lets assume you are promoting a product or service for consumers (B2C) or direct to business (B2B). Lets discuss a way you can come up with a list of social media campaigns that will result in an ongoing stream of conversation starters.

Brainstorm a list of topics of interest to your audience. No idea is a bad one. Now create a spreadsheet and list all the ideas. On the four columns to the right label each column; relevance, depth, market interest and knowledge.

1. **Relevance** - How relevant is the topic to your target audience.

2. **Depth** - How deep is the topic, can it be covered in a sentence or two or is it a rich topic with lots of interesting attributes that can be discussed, debated, researched and reported on over time.

3. **Market Interest** - How interesting is it to the marketplace. There are relevant topics in any industry that just aren't very interesting.

---

4. **Knowledge** - How much do you already know. This is a good indicator of how interested you are of the topics as well. Having knowledge and interest further ensures success of the campaign.

For each item on the list rate each column 1 to 5; five being the most of each topic. Add each row of scores to find out what topics get the highest scores. If your top score has tie scores you can prioritize and pick which one to do first.

In programming, you change one thing and test it. That way you know how your change effected the code. With social marketing campaigns we want to develop a campaign and then fine tune it over time. Campaigns can vary in steps and process but it should be documented and repeatable. Here's a simple campaign you can run on your first topic.

1. Creating content across channels - Your campaigns will consist of a variety of media and content used across social media sites to connect with your audience. For this example we'll try to hit some of the primary channels.

2. Start with a presentation - I usually start by making a quick PowerPoint presentation on the topic. This is where you can do all your primary research; be sure to share the research as you find it on Twitter, Facebook, LinkedIn etc.

Don't overdo it. Remember *Guy Kawasaki's 10/20/30 rule of PowerPoint presentations*:

• No more than 10 slides

• Not longer than 20 minutes

• Type size not less than 30 points

3. Take it on the road - After a few practice runs find a small group of people to present to. This could be a group at work, a rotary club, a local industry group or a college class. You will be surprised how quickly you can find a few people to present to. Bring a camera and have a friend take a few photos of the presentation and your audience.

4. Flickr - Upload the photos to Flickr with key word rich titles and descriptions; be sure to add them to your map so they are geo-tagged. This will help you improve your search engine results.

5. Blog the talk - Write a short blog entitled "XYZ Presentation at the Rotary Club"... Discuss how the presentation went and add a photo or slideshow from Flickr. Be sure to mention the location.

6. Create a video - Now you've had practice it's time to create a YouTube video. You can do this simply by talking through the slides to a cam corder, Flip camera or web cam. You can even record your presentation at a live event. I like to edit my slides into the video after recording.

It doesn't have to be perfect. I repeat - it doesn't have to be perfect. Practice this mantra "Done, not perfect". Now you can upload your video to YouTube. I like to use Blip.tv because it has the option to distribute your video content to a variety of sites including YouTube and iTunes.

7. Write the blog article - Now you should have enough insight and material to write a fantastic blog article. The piece need not be Moby Dick, but long enough to go slightly in-depth. You can reference people you've spoken with, share anecdotes, and be very familiar with the topic. You can embed your slides and/or video as well.

8. Promotion & Networking - Throughout this process, you and your team (if you have one) will be promoting and networking on behalf of the brand constantly.

Promotion

- Tweet everything; each new media element posted.

- Digg articles and content generated throughout the campaign. If you have time you can use other bookmarking sites such as Yahoo! Buzz and StumbleUpon as well.

- Post articles in multiple LinkedIn groups and LinkedIn status. But be careful not to be seen as one who engages in Spam.

- Post to Facebook and your Facebook fan page

Networking - You need to get to know and care about the community in your market.

You may want to subscribe to a variety of Google News searches. When you search on Google News or Google Blog Search you can subscribe to any of the results. You can set up a tab on your iGoogle home page to watch all your topic trends.

- Tweet content, retweet updates and converse on Twitter with your influencers. Promoting other people is a great way to make friends and increase buzz for your brand. It's human nature. If somebody mentions and promotes you and your brand, then a return of that favor is likely.

- Follow about 100 relevant people a day on Twitter. Products like Hootsuite can help you find people to follow; you can search members by keywords in their profile and/or updates. Its against the rules to use automated programs to follow and unfollow people but people do it. Just keep it under 100 per day - if you get caught your account can be suspended and/ or deleted.

- Digg articles for influencers. I'd suggest you seek Digg users that have had lots of articles on the front page and start Digging and Tweeting them. Build a network of Digg power users so you can send a message to your connections alerting them of new content you want Dugg.

- Comment on influencers blogs and fan pages

Its all about numbers

Woody Allen said "90 percent of life is just showing up". In order to show up as much as possible to generate buzz about your campaigns you need to show up in all the right places.

You need to optimize your content across social networks. Again, this is where a balance needs to be struck. Of course you want to gain customers, but in order to do so, trust is a premium. Thus, do not oversell. In fact, post content which speaks to your sector but does not mention your brand. To do this you will define an activity list for each content event. This way you can begin to measure how effective your activity is in gaining traffic.

Lets say you spend 4 hours a week promoting and networking and 25% of that time working with Twitter. You find 50% of your traffic comes from Twitter. You know that 1 hour a week generates 50% of your traffic. If you pay yourself $50 per hour that traffic cost $25 per week.

You can take it a step further. Lets say you get 10,000 unique visitors a month. for every 10,000 visitors you get .01% conversion rate or 100 leads. Of that 100 leads you get 2 sales on average. Each sale averages $10,000 dollars. Since you paid $25 to get half your traffic you know it cost $25 per Twitter lead. You can start to compare cost per lead across all your efforts. You may find yourself canceling a few direct mail projects.

Social Media Marketing

Social media marketing has become significant part of marketing efforts for major brands, here's some examples of successful campaigns.

Dell - Dell Computer has a strong blogging presence with its Direct2Dell forum. Not only is this a chance for bloggers to learn about new products but it has also helped improve the organizations' reputation. The amount of negative blogs dropped from 49% to 22% since the start of the site. Dell was able to connect with the customers and immediate address their concerns, comments, and questions through the blog.

Target - Target has been successful on Facebook by "getting real" with customers and exposing products which resonate with the customers. Target took time to understand the medium and how to use it to benefit connecting with the customer. They embraced the learning curve and did especially well by allowing customers to help shape the group.

Starbucks - Starbucks can be found on Facebook, You-Tube, Flickr, Twitter, and on their own blogging site My Starbucks Idea. Starbucks is considered to have one of the best social media strategies. The focus is geared toward the needs, wants and likes of existing companies and building that relationship to help gain new customers.

Being Authentic

We've seen in sitcoms the pick-up artist borrowing a puppy or babysitting a toddler to attract women and have an instant conversation opener. We need to be authentic in the activities that we participate in to generate brand awareness. You may get away with some self-serving activity, but get found out and you'll be paying for it.

What do you call a phony blog that's actually a front for a huge corporation? A "flog"?

A pro-Wal-Mart blog called "Wal-Marting Across America," ostensibly launched by a pair of average Americans chronicling their cross-country travels in an RV and lodging in Wal-Mart parking lots, has been reduced to a farewell entry. One of its two contributors was revealed to be Jim Thresher, a staff photographer for The Washington Post.

The blog, launched Sept. 27, was profiled in Businessweek, which exposed the site as a promotional tactic engineered by Working Families for Wal-Mart (WFWM), an organization launched by Edelman, Wal-Mart's public relations firm.. WFWM paid for the RV and all travel expenses, rerouted the trip's original plan, and plastered a logo on the RV's side. Though a banner ad announced WFWM sponsored the site, it did not divulge Wal-Mart paid for the couple's RV, gas, food and other expenses.

Friends with Benefits

We can guess our pick-up artist isn't interested in a committed relationship. The golden cup for him is for he and his conquest to become "Friends with Benefits". This means they can continue with their bedroom activity with "no strings attached (NSA)".

The same holds true for marketers. The brand and the customer need to stay friends, add value to each other's lives and continue to have a mutually beneficial relationship. Just because someone isn't using my product now doesn't mean we can't be friends. That way at the moment of - CUTS OFF

The Long Tail

The Long Tail is a theory of statistical probability which suggests because of the great reach of technology there are

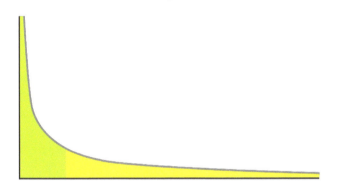

An example of a power law graph showing popularity ranking. To the right is the long tail; to the left are the few that dominate. Notice that the areas of both regions match.

The Long Tail describes the "three driving forces" that you must understand to master it...

1. Tools Of Production - Hardware and software put product creation into the hands of everyone. For example, camcorders enable millions of budding Tarentinos. Software empowers people to share their knowledge in the form of Web sites and blogs. The result? An exponential explosion in niche products.

Of course, these tools don't guarantee quality. There is a lot of bad video "out there." Nor do they put your high-value niche products into the hands of those who want it.

2. The Internet Aggregators - Aggregators pull "products" together, offering all in one spot. For example, iTunes aggregates music, offering an easy one-stop destination to consumers. Google AdSense pulls publishers together -- in this case, the product is the Web site. Advertisers from General Motors to Stan's Local Body Shop can filter through Google's aggregation of publishers and place ads across a wide variety of sites related to what they want to sell.

3. Filtering Software - This links supply and demand This enables consumers to find those high-quality, produced(#1)-and-aggregated(#2) niche products. For example, are you planning a vacation to Anguilla? Do a Google search to find great sites about Anguilla. See the ads on those sites? Click! Your interest earns income for both Google and the site-publisher.

Your Little Black Book

Wether you are email marketing or calling prospects, your customer list is the lifeline of your business. If you

---

aren't already, from this day forward every campaign, event, special offer or any kind of marketing tactic should be aimed at one thing and one thing only. Building the list or what we call conversion. Its the "little black book" of marketing success.

Customer reviews and other forms of word of mouth, often referred to as testimonials, make great fodder for e-mail campaigns. When measured against identical campaigns these peer to peer pull quotes, they generally drive higher click-through rates and sales. Two key benefits of e-mail and user-generated content include driving community participation and using trusted words of customers to market products.For retailers, e-mails that feature "top-rated products" or "customer favorites" and include actual customer ratings or review content snippets see much better result than those without this transparent content.

eSpares, the UK's largest appliance spare parts retailer, found that a link to customer reviews in e-mails outperformed all other links in its e-mail, including other text-based links and a "buy now" button. In addition, incremental traffic to the Web site from the "read reviews" link ended up generating additional revenue, 2.5 times that sold through the "buy now" button.

E-mail infused with authentic customer opinions adds a level of credibility and engagement that is seldom matched by other types of content.

Managing the list

You may use a full blown customer relationship management (CRM) system or something as simple as MailChimp, and email list management tool. You are always trying to get another number, or in our case an email address. This allows us to recontact the prospect, to keep in touch and take the relationship to the next level.

MailChimp is a low-cost, easy to use email marketing tool

It's smart to start with something simple that can export your list. Bloated CRM systems can slow you down and create bottlenecks. Marketers should be hands on with their lists.

Once you have a sizable list you can do nifty things to test your campaigns. Certain headings, graphics, call to action buttons can have varying results. One great trick is to use A/B testing. Use a segment of your list, about 10% of the total recipients. Send half one version and send the other half a slightly different version. Whichever has the best open and click rates send that version to the rest of your list.

Word of Mouth

Word of Mouth (WOM) marketing is how companies can get new customers through recommendations. The fact is that people love to discover things and when they find something valuable it brings them pleasure to pass it along.

I've purchased things I didn't even know I needed because a trusted friend encouraged me to do so. "Hey Dean, you are going to love this new wireless headset" my friend Frank texted me via Skype. Next came a link, followed by a conversation. I hit the "buy with 1-click" button on Amazon and three days later I have a new headset that I've used 3 or 4 times in the past month.

With blogs, instant messaging text messages, social networks, and discussion forums its become easy to tell people what you bought. Just about every shopping site has links to Tweet or post the item on Facebook. Websites often provide referral incentives, if you refer a certain number of people you get a free month membership, credits or discounts.

All word of mouth marketing techniques are based on the concepts of customer satisfaction, two-way dialogue, and transparent communications. The basic elements are:

- Educating people about your products and services

- Identifying people most likely to share their opinions

- Providing tools that make it easier to share information

- Studying how, where, and when opinions are being shared

- Listening and responding to supporters, detractors, and neutrals

Fine tuning performance

The beauty of social marketing is the availability of data. Like the proverbial notches on the belt of our pick

up artist, there are various ways to keep score and care-
fully monitor how your campaign might be working, or
not.

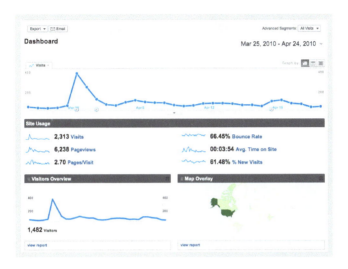

Absolute Unique Visitors are the number of unique
individuals who've come to your site in a given time
period. So, if I come to your site 20 times in a week, I
still only count as a single unique visitor. This statistic
is important because it tells you your reach, or the total
size of the audience coming to your site.

Visits are the number of times folks open your site in
their browser. If I come to your site 20 times in a week, I
count as 20 visits. This is important, too - a high ratio of
visits to visitors means you've got a loyal audience.

Page Views tell you how many pages of your site are viewed in a given period. If I come to your site 20 times in a week, viewing 3 pages each time, I count as 60 page views. Page views are an indication of just how interested folks are in your site. A high ratio of page views to visits likely means an interested audience.

Finally, Referring Source, found under Visitor Segment Performance, tells you where folks are coming from. And, you can use the Analysis button to drill further down, viewing keywords searched, etc...

Concluding Thoughts

It's time to get hip to the social marketplace. If you want to build meaningful relationships and be able to score with customers you need to up your game. The pick-up artist can't walk right up to a prospect and start describing his "special attributes" or pointing out the defining properties of the prospect. The marketer needs to focus on building long-term relationships, creating referral networks and adding value all along the way.

The social media marketplace is transparent and the best tactic is no tactic at all. There's discipline in adding real value and distributing content across channels. There's the discipline of constantly looking for ways to improve your customers experience.

An old salesman explained to a young trainee. "A good salesman will ask lots of questions, remember things about their prospects, check up on them. A better salesman will show caring by sending birthday cars and providing things the prospect likes; baseball cards, fruit baskets, coffee cups. A great salesman actually love his prospects and do what comes natural."

About Dean Whitney

A pioneer in interactive media, Dean Whitney is the Founder and Principal of Dean Whitney Interactive. He oversees all strategy, user experience and development using systems and processes developed over 15 years of experience.

Dean was an early adopter of Web 2.0 and a social media evangel-ist at integrated brand advertising agency Digitas. Prior to Digitas headed technology start-ups and online marketing groups at global Fortune 100 companies.

Dean is involved in many start-ups and organizations as an advisor and board director.

Dean is a sought after speaker, a blogger and has worked with many of the world's most recognized brands including Cisco, Fidelity, GM, Microsoft, Royal Caribbean and collaborated with top agencies such as Leo Burnett, JWT, Saatchi & Saatchi and Starcom.

On Twitter @deanwhit

See his blog: deanwhitney.com/blog

www.ingramcontent.com/pod-product-compliance
Lightning Source LLC
Chambersburg PA
CBHW041147050326
40689CB00001B/520